Freezer Meals

33 Quick and Easy Make Ahead Meals Your Whole Family Will Love

Sara Elliott Price

Published in The USA by:
Success Life Publishing
125 Thomas Burke Dr.
Hillsborough, NC 27278

Copyright © 2015 by Sara Elliott Price

ISBN-10: 1511871571

ALL RIGHTS RESERVED. No part of this publication may be reproduced or transmitted in any form whatsoever, electronic, or mechanical, including photocopying, recording, or by any informational storage or retrieval system without the express written permission from the author, except for the use of brief quotations in a book review.

Disclaimer

Every effort has been made to accurately represent this book and its potential. Results vary with every individual, and your results may or may not be different from those depicted. No promises, guarantees or warranties, whether stated or implied, have been made that you will produce any specific result from this book. Your efforts are individual and unique, and may vary from those shown. Your success depends on your efforts, background and motivation.

The material in this publication is provided for educational and informational purposes only and is not intended as medical advice. The information contained in this book should not be used to diagnose or treat any illness, metabolic disorder, disease or health problem. Always consult your physician or health care provider before beginning any nutrition or exercise program. Use of the programs, advice, and information contained in this book is at the sole choice and risk of the reader.

Table of Contents

Introduction 1

Mastering the Basics of Freezer Meals 3
    Planning for the cooking session 3
    Options for packaging 5
    Tips for packaging, sealing and labelling 8
    Texture changes post freezing 10
    Points to Remember when freezing 12
    Preparing food before cooking and freezing 13
    Blanching vegetables 15
    Freezing fruits 19
    Treating fish, poultry and red meat 21

Meat Recipes 23
    Honey Lime Chicken 24
    Chicken Pot Pie 26
    Chicken Enchiladas 28
    Lasagna 30
    Orange-Sesame Turkey Cutlets 32
    Island Chicken with Pineapple Salsa 34
    Lentil-Rice Stew with Turkey Sausage 36
    Chicken Mac & Cheese 38
    Beef Stew with Creamy Mashed Potatoes 40

Vegetarian Recipes 42
    Handy tips for roasting vegetables 42
    Mexican Quinoa 44
    Baked Ziti With Roasted Veggies 46

Vegetable Soup...47
  Cheese Stuffed Peppers..49
  Basil and Vegetable Soup..51
  Vegetables and Chili 53
  Vegetable Jambalaya Casserole 55
  Chili Rice Casseroles..57
  Noodle Casserole with Sour Cream 58

Fish Recipes 60
  Cod with Salsa Verde...61
  Sweet Sicilian Halibut..63
  Curry-spiced Seafood with Veggies and Rice............65

Snack Recipes...67
  Shrimp Puffs 67
  Filo Onion Rolls 69
  Calzones 71
  Jalapeno Poppers 73
  Red and White Tortellini 75

Dessert Recipes 76
  Tips for freezing and thawing desserts......................76
  Mud Pie - Mocha edition 77
  Pumpkin Pie..78
  Strawberry Lemon Mousse Tartlets 80
  Coffee Almond Tart 81

Breakfast Recipes 82
  Stuffed Italian Burgers 82
  Apricot and Raisin Oatmeal...84
  Hearty & Healthy Blueberry Muffins 85

Conclusion...87

Introduction

Cooking ahead and freezing prepared meals for later is the best method available to preserve cooked food and its nutrients, colors and flavors all while avoiding having to cook before eating. It can be a great way to eat healthy for busy moms, people in professions like trucking, individuals on a budget and even a great option if you are trying to stay on a specific diet for long periods of time. Cooking ahead and freezing meals has many advantages.

Whether you're at home alone, too busy to cook, expecting more guests than you can cook for, too lazy, or simply want to maximize the results of the effort you put in, cooking ahead is the thing to do. I'm sure we could all find some use for more time in our lives. Just think, haven't there been times when you said to yourself, that "I wish I didn't have to cook now?" other than these circumstances mentioned above, there are many other reasons why cooking ahead makes sense.

Some of these reasons are:

- Saves work, time and money
- Is an efficient and easy method of preserving food

- Can simplify the process of meal preparation
- Provides delicious meals at a moment's notice
- Supplies you with seasonal favorites even after the season is over
- You have to make fewer, planned shopping trips
- Allows you to stock up on special sales while prices are low
- Allows you to use your oven more efficiently, baking more than one dish at a time

I'm a big fan of cooking ahead and I do so to make the most of my time while eating planned, wholesome and delicious meals quickly. Since I work from home, cook ahead meals mean that we only have to cook once a day now. Sometimes, when I have a very busy week ahead I'll prepare a whole weeks' worth of food ahead of time. The concept of cook ahead meals has saved the day for my family many times.

Mastering the Basics of Freezer Meals

Planning for the cooking session

Plan your menu a few days before shopping and cooking days. When cooking meals in large batches to freeze, always start with recipes you know and love. It is generally not advisable to experiment with new recipes when starting out.

Pick 3-4 recipes and get started. You can add more recipes to your repertoire as you gradually get the hang of freezer cooking. Getting in to the groove will be easy.

Schedule two blocks of time for freezer cooking. The first block of time is to shop for all the Ingredients and the second block to prepare and cook everything.

Plan the cooking session before you start. You need to wash and Blanche vegetables, treat all fruits with ascorbic acid and cut and prepare all the ingredients, including meat and poultry items. You also need to prepare all spices and condiments, have all the creams and sauces ready, and finally, cook your recipes.

<u>Assemble your recipes</u> like an assembly line if it's going to be a long session with multiple types of meals.

<u>Organize recipes by ingredients.</u> Before starting the cooking session get all ingredients handy. Play some music. Get going.

Options for packaging

<u>Vacuum sealers</u> are great for long-term storage. These come with bags and the vacuum sealer can suck the air out of the package and get a nice tight wrap. These bags are transparent and allow you to see what is inside the package. It's ideal if you buy meat and produce in bulk and store them in your freezer.

<u>If you do not use a vacuum sealer, you may try this</u>: To take out as much air as possible, zip the bag almost closed, leaving about one inch open and put a straw into the opening, zip the bag tight around the straw, and suck as much air as possible out of the bag through the straw. Quickly pull out the straw and zip the bag fully. You can also try out the new zip-top bags with double walls, especially designed to prevent freezer burn.

<u>Silicone pans</u> are an option. These can withstand extreme temperatures and are suitable for freezing your food and can go straight in the oven as well. These are easy to use and clean but can also be wobbly, so a cookie sheet is advised. Since silicone pans are flexible it becomes easy to pop out frozen food and store them in freezer bags so that you can reuse the pan.

Freezer zip-top bags are useful for marinated meats, baked goods, and other items that hold on to their own shape. You can use these for stews, soups, and beans as well, but the leakage is a factor to consider. One great thing about zip-top bags is that they can lie flat, be lined up like books on a shelf. You can keep them any way you choose to. They can store lots of food in small spaces. You can reuse these bags in some cases. Reusing bags that have stored raw meat is not advised.

Reusable plastic containers with lids are great for storing liquids, sauces, soups, and stews. Storing shredded chicken and taco meat in these containers makes reheating easier.

Disposable aluminum baking pans can be difficult to clean, making them hard to reuse. But, they can be extremely convenient, especially for giving meals as gifts or taking them to potlucks, and other such uses.

Glass or metal baking dishes last the longest. It might hurt having all your pans sitting in the freezer when you need to cook something fresh. However, if you have a large supply, go for it.

You can use aluminum foil, transparent film bags and other methods for packing as well.

The packaging material must be:
- Airtight
- Moisture-proof
- Odor-proof
- Vapor-proof

You can choose any kind of packaging material you like. As always experience is your best teacher in learning what works best for you.

Tips for packaging, sealing and labelling

- Select containers according to the thawing and reheating needs for each food. For example: Use microwave ready material when the food can be instantly heated to eat.
- Cooling any food and/or syrups before packing speeds up freezing and helps to retain natural flavor, color and texture of food.
- Pack foods in quantities designed to be used at one time.
- Most food needs some head room between the packed food and the closure, as food expands as it freezes. Loose packing items such as asparagus, broccoli, tray-packed foods, breads, and bony pieces of meat, do not need any head space.
- Pack foods tightly to cut down on the amount of air in the package.
- Run a non-metallic utensil such as a rubber scraper handle around the inside of the package to eliminate air pockets.
- When wrapping your food, make sure you press out as much air as possible and mold the wrapping around the food as tight as possible. The more oxygen that is forced out of the packet, the better the quality of food will be when eating.
- Before packing food in bags, press air out of the bags, press firmly beginning with the bottom of the bag first, moving to

the top of the bag to prevent air from re-entering. You may force the air out by putting the filled and sealed bag in a bowl of cold water. Seal it by twisting it, using a rubber band, other sealing device, or a strip of coated wire.

- Keep the sealing edges free from food or moisture for a good closure.
- When using tape, ensure it is freezer tape and designed for use in a freezer. The adhesive in this type of tape remains effective at lower temperatures.
- Label all containers with the name of the product, amount and date. You may use freezer marking crayons, pens or gummed labels if you want to.
- Keep an inventory of the freezer meals available and check an item off once you eat it. This simply lets you know when to cook a new batch.

Texture changes post freezing

Food of almost any kind will undergo some changes after freezing. For instance, mayonnaise, cooked egg and cream-based salad dressings will separate when frozen alone. Potatoes darken and have a change in texture when included in frozen soups and stews. New potatoes freeze better than older ones.

Below are some other changes that should be considered when freezing meals.

- Soft meringues shrink and toughen.
- Cooked egg whites turn tough and rubbery.
- Gravies thickened with wheat-flour, and milk sauces can curdle or separate.
- Half-and-half, sour cream, buttermilk, cottage cheese and yogurt may separate and become watery or grainy when frozen alone.
- Cream fillings and custard separate and can become watery and lumpy.
- Cooked pasta loses texture and tends to taste different when frozen by itself.

- Most gelatin based dishes 'weep' when thawed.
- Crumbs or cheese toppings get soggy.
- High water content vegetables like celery, lettuce, cucumbers, tomatoes, parsley, radishes become watery and limp.
- Canned hams tend to get watery and tough.
- Stuffed poultry should not be frozen. It does not freeze well.

Points to Remember when freezing

Expect some changes in the seasoning level of frozen dishes. Season sparingly, it is best to season to taste when the food is reheated.

- Add any crumb or cheese toppings right before reheating. These can get soggy when frozen.
- If possible, slightly undercook food to allow some additional cooking while reheating. Some experimenting is necessary to perfect this technique.
- Quickly cool the food that you want frozen by placing the container of hot food into a sink or pan of ice water.
- Baking dishes should be lined with plastic wrap or foil, and then removed and properly wrapped for freezer storage.

Preparing food before cooking and freezing

Before cooking and freezing, fruits and vegetables must be washed thoroughly. You can cleanse them by rinsing in several changes of clean water. Most berries only require a gentle rinse. Avoid soaking fruits or vegetables in water for too long as soaking tends to remove valuable nutrients.

I personally mix 1/3 cup vinegar in a sink full of water to rinse my produce. This is the absolute best way to clean your produce of dirt, pesticides, etc.

Freezing, heating, and treating with chemical compounds influences enzyme reactions. Freezing slows down activity of enzymes so that frozen foods will be fine with no further treatment.

Enzymes are deactivated by heat in vegetables during the process of blanching. In fruits, enzymes causes browning and loss of vitamin C, and can be regulated by chemical compounds (antioxidants like ascorbic acid).

Washing fruits and vegetables properly will:

- Remove microorganisms from the surface
- Remove dirt from the surface
- Remove pesticide residues
- Helps you avoid insects, eggs and larvae
- Better visibility after proper washing aids in removal of bruises so they are trimmed out

Blanching vegetables is the best treatment possible before cooking. Other than green pepper and onions, almost all other vegetables are known to maintain better quality in freezer storage after blanching (or heated enough to deactivate enzymes) before freezing.

Why Blanch Vegetables?

- Blanching stops or in some cases slows the action of enzymes that usually cause loss of texture, flavor, color and nutrients.
- Blanching will cleanse dirt and organisms from the surface.
- Blanching softens and/or wilts vegetables, which makes filling the containers easier.

Blanching time varies among different kinds of vegetables. Under blanching vegetables stimulates the activity of enzymes and is actually worse than no blanching at all. Over-blanching, on the other hand, will cause an unnecessary loss of color, flavor, minerals and vitamins.

The blanching times for individual vegetables are shared starting on the next page.

VEGETABLES	BLANCHING TIME (in boiling water in minutes unless otherwise mentioned)
Asparagus (Stalks)	
Small	2
Medium	3
Large	4
Artichoke	
Globe (Hearts)	7
Jerusalem	3–5
Beans–Green, Wax, or snap	3
Beans–Pinto, Lima, or Butter	
Small	2
Medium	3
Large	4
Beets	cook
Broccoli	
Floweret's 1½ inches	3
If Steamed	5
Brussel Sprouts (Heads)	
Small	3
Medium	4
Large	5
Cabbage (Shredded)	1.5
Carrots	
Small	5
Sliced, Diced or Strips	2
Cauliflower	

Flowerets, 1 inch	3
Corn	
(Ears)	
Small	7
Medium	9
Large	11
Cream Style or Whole Kernel	4
(Blanch ears before cutting from cob)	
Eggplant	4
Kohlrabi	
Cubes	1
Whole	3
Mushrooms (Steamed)	
Whole	9
Quarters or buttons	9
Slices	5
Okra (Pods)	
Small	3
Large	5
Peas	
Edible pods	2-3
Field (blackeye)	2
Green	1.5-2.5
Sweet Peppers	
Halves	3
Rings or Strips	2
Pumpkin	Cook

Rutabagas	3
Soybeans	5
Squash Summer winter	2 cook
Turnips or Parsnips Cubed	2

Freezing fruits: What blanching is to vegetables, dipping fruits in a solution of ascorbic acid is to fruits. Some fruits like apples, peaches, apricots and pears darken quickly once exposed to air and during freezing. These fruits also sometimes lose flavor when thawed. The cut surface of the fruit usually contains enzymes, which tend to discolor (turn brown) when exposed to air.

When preparing fruit for storage, dip fruit for about 2 minutes in a solution of ascorbic acid before freezing. The fruits may be halved, peeled, quartered, diced or sliced prior to dipping. This method also prevents stem-end discoloration in fruits like cherries and grapes.

You can find ascorbic acid in various forms at your local supermarket.

<u>Pure powdered form</u> — seasonally available in the canning supply section in most supermarkets. One level teaspoon of pure powder weighs around three grams and you can use one teaspoon for a gallon of water to make a treatment solution.

<u>Vitamin C tablets</u> — These are very economical and available

year round. You most likely will find 500-milligram tablets. To use, crush and dissolve about six 500 mg tablets in a gallon of water and use as a treatment solution.

Commercially prepared mixtures of citric acid and ascorbic acid— Seasonally available in the canning supply section. Citric acid powder is sold in supermarkets, but it is less effective in controlling discoloration. Also, citric acid may lend a sour taste to preserved fruits. If you choose to use these be sure to follow the manufacturer's directions.

Treating fish, poultry and red meat properly can be a very important aspect of cooking freezer meals. Some general tips are given below.

- Freeze meat as soon after slaughter as possible to ensure its freshness and quality.
- Trim excess fat and remove bones if possible, and cover sharp extruding bones with foil or folded freezer paper so they do not pierce the wrapper.
- Freeze meat in meal-size pieces and package
- Vacuum-packaged meats can be frozen in the undamaged package for one to three months.
- Freezer bags or containers should be used for freezing stew meats, ground meats or other meats frozen into small portions.
- Red meat will turn dark or pale brown. This does not mean it is spoiled, it is simply from oxygen exposure.
- Don't add emulsifiers (like mayonnaise) to meat. Slow freezing creates large ice crystals in the meat. When thawing, they damage the cells and emulsions get dissolved. This makes meat "drip" and lose its juiciness. Emulsions such as mayonnaise or cream will separate and appear curdled.
- Cooked meat, poultry or casseroles may be cooked or

reheated once frozen. However, it takes roughly one and a half times longer to cook. Don't forget to discard any wraps or absorbing paper from meat or poultry before you cook.
- Leave fish as a whole or in large pieces if it is to be stored longer than three months.
- Wash fish thoroughly. If slime is an issue, rinse in a solution of one teaspoon vinegar to three quarts of cold water.
- Clean fish immediately and freeze as soon as possible.
- To decrease rancidity and flavor change, place fatty kinds of fish in a dip of ascorbic acid for 20 seconds (the ratio of the dip: 2 tablespoons ascorbic acid to 1 quart cold water).
- Immerse lean types of fish in a chilled salt water - ¼ cup salt to 1 quart water for 20 minutes. This firms the fish up and minimizes drip loss when thawed.
- One of the best methods of wrapping fish is with a clinging plastic wrap and then overwrap it in freezer wrap. Squeeze out as much air as possible, less oxygen, better fish. Place the fish in freezer bags, seal and submerge in a pan of cold water to force air out. Apply a seal tape if possible.
- Keep fish in the coolest corner of the freezer.

Meat Recipes

Here are some tips on freezing cooked chicken or other meats:

- Freeze shredded chicken in portions of 1 cup, then label with spices and flavors that were used while cooking.
- If reheating leftovers, retain moisture and make sure chicken is heated fully by covering. Before serving make sure gravies are brought to a rolling boil.
- To transport cooked chicken, place it in an insulated container until ready to enjoy. Keep chicken at 40°F or below or make sure it's above 140°F.

Honey Lime Chicken

Ingredients:

- 4 chicken breasts cut into strips
- 1 T oil of choice
- 1½ t garlic salt
- 1 20 Oz can pineapple tidbits, keep juice
- 2 T soy sauce
- 2 t corn starch
- ¼ C honey
- 3 T lime juice

Preparation:

1. Sprinkle strips or bite sized pieces of chicken with garlic salt.
2. Heat oil over medium to high on a skillet.
3. Add chicken and cook until golden brown.
4. Drain the can of pineapple, but keep the juice.
5. Add ¼ C of pineapple juice to the heated skillet and cover then simmer for 6-8 minutes.
6. Take the chicken away from the skillet and add lime juice, honey, soy sauce, corn starch and the rest of the pineapple juice to the pan.
7. Stir constantly and bring to a boil.
8. Stir and cook until it's thick and clear, should take around 1 minute.

9. Now put pineapple tidbits and chicken in last and heat it through.
10. Best served over hot rice with a garnishment of lime wedges.
11. When freezing this recipe, make sure to cook as directed. Let it cool, put into a freezer bag, then label the bags and freeze. When ready to use simply heat it and serve with hot, fresh rice.

Chicken Pot Pie

Ingredients:

- Homemade chicken stock gravy (or use 2 cans of Campbell's chicken gravy)
- 2 C cooked chicken, shredded
- 2 pie Crust (purchased or homemade)
- Onion, ¼ cup diced small
- 16 Oz frozen hash browns (diced)
- Frozen Peas & Carrots
- Salt and pepper as desired

Preparation:

1. Preheat your oven to 350.
2. Bring out the pie crusts. If purchased take one of the tins out and thaw on counter and turn the other tin upside down as it thaws.
3. While it is thawing, mix everything together in a bowl the hash browns, shredded chicken, peas, carrots, onion and gravy.
4. Add salt and pepper as desired.
5. Once the crust has thawed (takes 15 minutes), add the Ingredients: in the bowl to the pie crust.
6. Take the upside down crust and carefully place it on top of the other gently. Pinch the pie crusts together.
7. Poke some holes with a fork or knife on top.

8. Cover to freeze, or place in a 350 degree oven and cook for the next 35-45 minutes. It's done when the top is golden brown and you hear it bubbling.

Chicken Enchiladas

Ingredients:

- 4 Chicken Breasts
- 3 C Cheddar Cheese, Shredded
- 1 Medium Onion, diced
- 2 Cans Red Enchilada Sauce
- 10 Medium Flour Tortillas
- Optional:
- 1 Can Black Beans
- Jalapenos
- White Rice

Preparation:

1. Preheat the oven to 350 degrees.
2. Put chicken breasts into a pot of water.
3. Boil for 20 minutes, or until chicken is easily shreddable.
4. Shred the chicken on a cutting board.
5. Mix onion, cheese, chicken and 1 can of enchilada sauce in a bowl. Add the optional Ingredients: now if desired.
6. With a large spoon, fill each tortilla with Ingredients: in bowl. Roll them up and put them in a large baking dish Place rolled tortillas in dish with the seams down.
7. Use the second can of enchilada sauce to pour on top of tortillas.

8. Place cheese on top.
9. Bake for 25 - 30 minutes, till melted and bubbly.
10. Serve with salsa, sour cream, lettuce beans and rice.

Lasagna

Ingredients:

- 1lb. Ground beef
- 1 med. Onion, chopped
- 1 16 Oz Spaghetti Sauce
- 1 pint Cottage Cheese
- 12 Oz shredded Mozzarella Cheese
- 4 Oz Lasagna Noodles(cook al dente and cool in cold water)
- ¼ C grated Parmesan cheese
- ½ t Salt
- ⅛ t Garlic powder
- 2 T dried Parsley

Preparation:

Mix ground beef, garlic powder, salt and onion. Cook on med/high until browned. Drain mixture and toss back into the skillet. Add the spaghetti sauce and begin simmering for about 15 minutes. Make sure to stir on occasion.

In a bowl add cottage cheese, Parmesan cheese and the dried parsley. Toss well.

Layering Lasagna

1. First add and spread a tiny amount of spaghetti sauce mixture onto the bottom of the pan to prevent sticking.
2. Layer one row of noodles
3. Layer sauce - ⅓
4. Layer mozzarella cheese - ⅓
5. Layer cheese mixture all over - ⅓
6. Layer one row of noodles
7. Layer sauce - ⅓
8. Layer mozzarella cheese - ⅓
9. Layer cheese mixture all over - ⅓
10. Layer 1 row of noodles
11. Layer sauce - ⅓
12. Layer cheese mixture all over - ⅓
13. Layer mozzarella cheese on top - ⅓

Cover and place in a 350 degree oven and bake for 40-45 minutes. It should be golden brown and bubbly. Take out of oven and let sit for 10 minutes.

To freeze simply cut into slices, cover and freeze. When reheating, take out of freezer and take desired amount and heat in a 350 degree oven for 10 minutes.

Orange-Sesame Turkey Cutlets

Ingredients:

- 1lb turkey cutlets
- 1 C orange juice
- 1 T soy sauce
- 1 t corn starch
- 1 t garlic, minced
- 3/4 C defatted chicken stock, thawed
- 1 T minced fresh cilantro
- 1 t dark sesame oil

Preparation:

1. In a shallow non-metal dish, mix orange juice, oil, soy sauce and garlic. Add in turkey. Cover and place in the refrigerator for an hour, turn frequently in between.
2. Heat a non-stick skillet with cooking spray, and heat on med/high till hot.
3. Add turkey in one layer. Cook for 2 minutes on 1 side, then 2 minutes on the other side. They should be golden brown. Put turkey aside on a plate, cover to keep turkey warm.
4. Place corn starch in a bowl.
5. Add chicken stock and stir the mixture until well mixed.
6. Add marinade, combine well and cut the heat to medium.
7. Pour into the heated skillet.

8. Stir and cook until the sauce has become thickened, usually for 3 minutes.
9. Add the turkey and cook for another 4-6 minutes. Make sure the turkey isn't pink in the middle. Insert the tip of a knife into a cutlet to check if cooked.
10. Sprinkle with cilantro and serve over quinoa or rice.

To freeze: Simply place cooled cutlets and sauce in a quality freezer container.

To use: Place in refrigerator and thaw overnight. Microwave for 5 minutes, or till it's hot.

Island Chicken with Pineapple Salsa

Ingredients:

- 8 Oz crushed un-sweetened pineapple (keep juice)
- 1 T reduced-sodium soy sauce
- 2 cloves garlic, minced
- 1 T honey
- 1/4 t crushed red pepper
- 4-6 Oz chicken breast halves, skinned and boned
- 1/4 C packed brown sugar
- 1/2 C diced onions
- 1 t minced fresh cilantro
- 2 T lime juice
- 1 t minced jalapeno peppers

Preparation:

1. Strain the pineapple and keep the juice. Put the pineapple in a bowl, cover and refrigerate.
2. Put the pineapple juice in a pan. Add some soy sauce, garlic, honey, and red-pepper flakes and combine well. Add chicken and toss it so mixture is coated onto chicken.
3. Cover and refrigerate for 4-24 hours, occasionally turning it.
4. Preheat the grill and spray the grill rack or pan with cooking spray.

5. Get the bowl of pineapple. Add brown sugar, onions, jalapeno peppers, lime juice and cilantro. Combine well. Leave at room temperature.
6. Remove the chicken from the marinade and keep the marinade. Simply grill or broil 4 in. from the heat for about 5 minutes on each side. Insert the tip of a knife into a cutlet to check if cooked, make sure pink is gone.
7. Transfer the marinade to a saucepan. Boil over med/high heat. Cook 5 minutes, or reduced to half. Pour marinade over the chicken and place salsa on top.

To freeze: Place cooled cutlets in freezer in a freezer-approved dish.

To use: Thaw overnight in a refrigerator. Microwave for 3-5 minutes, or till it's hot. Remember to top with salsa.

Lentil-Rice Stew with Turkey Sausage

Ingredients:

- 8 Oz low fat Italian turkey sausage
- 2 C green cabbage, chopped
- 1 t curry powder
- 1 C dried lentils
- 2 T minced fresh parsley
- 1 C onions, chopped
- 1 green pepper, chopped
- 3 garlic cloves, minced
- 4 C defatted chicken stock
- 1/2 C Rice
- 1/4 t black pepper, ground

Preparation:

1. Spray cooking spray in a Dutch oven and put on medium to high heat till hot.
2. Add sausage. Cook and Stir for 5 minutes, till browned.
3. Add onions, cabbage, garlic, green peppers and a cup of stock. Stir for 5 minutes, onions should be soft but not yet browned.
4. Add curry powder, rice, lentils, and remaining stock, boil on medium.

5. Cover and continue cooking, occasionally stirring for the next 25 minutes, the lentils should be soft while the stew will be thick.
6. Add parsley and black pepper, mix well.

To use: Take out of freezer and thaw in the fridge overnight and place in a covered saucepan. Stir frequently until hot.

Chicken Mac & Cheese

Ingredients:

- 6 chicken breasts or thighs, boneless and skinless
- 16 Oz elbow noodles
- 16 Oz Monterrey Jack cheese, grated
- 2 C chicken stock
- 2- 10.75 Oz cans cream of mushroom soup
- 2 cloves garlic, chopped
- 1/2 C onion, chopped
- 3 T mayonnaise
- 3/4 C chopped pimento pepper
- 1 sleeve Ritz crackers, crushed

Preparation:

1. Preheat oven to 350 degrees.
2. Boil chicken in a large stock pot covered with water for 20 minutes on medium heat. Remove the chicken from the stock and let it cool.
3. Pour the noodles into the pot and continue cooking on medium heat for 10 minutes. Chop the chicken into small pieces. Once noodles are al dente, drain the chicken stock and keep it for later.
4. Add noodles, chicken, and the remaining Ingredients: to a mixing bowl and stir well.

5. Pour into two casserole pans(9x13).
6. Cover with Ritz Crackers on top.
7. Bake in the preheated oven for 30 minutes.

To freeze: Wrap tightly with aluminum foil and store in the freezer.

To use: Thaw overnight before cooking. If you are planning to bake it frozen, place it in the oven while it preheats and give it about 10 to 20 minutes extra cooking time to make sure it is properly heated.

Beef Stew with Creamy Mashed Potatoes

Ingredients:

- 1 T butter
- 2lbsstew meat, cut in chunks
- 3 garlic cloves
- 1 diced medium onion
- 4 Oz tomato paste
- Worcestershire sauce
- 4 C beef broth
- 4 carrots, diced
- 2 turnips peeled and diced
- 2 T parsley
- 1/2 t sugar
- 3 T olive oil

Preparation:

1. Stew meat with salt and pepper.
2. Warm the olive oil in a pot and set burner to medium heat.
3. Add the butter. Once it melts, fry the meat until it's brown, around 2 minutes (keep turning the sides). Remove the beef and stock.
4. Fry garlic and onion until the onion is light brown.
5. Add tomato paste and stir fry for 2 minutes.
6. Pour in the beef stock; keep stirring constantly all the while.

7. Add Worcestershire and sugar.
8. Add beef and cover, let simmer for 90 minutes to 2 hours.
9. After the 2 or so hours, throw in the turnips and carrots. Stir and re-cover stew. Simmer for additional 30 minutes.
10. Once turnips and carrots are cooked through, add parsley. Last, salt and pepper as needed.

Freeze in a freezer compatible bag until ready to serve. Serve with mashed potatoes.

Vegetarian Recipes

Handy tips for roasting vegetables

ONE AT A TIME: Roast one vegetable at a time since all vegetables require different cooking times.

OVEN TEMPERATURE: Roast vegetables at high temperature, 400F to 450F.

SAME SIZE: While the oven preheats, prep the vegetables. Blanche and trim the vegetables removing any blemishes, cut off stems and tails, removing skins when appropriate. Then cut the vegetables into similarly sized pieces. The smaller the pieces, the quicker will they roast, and the larger they are, the longer they take.

SHRINKAGE: Vegetables shrink when they are roasted so do allow for that.

SEASONING: A vegetable's own natural flavor will emerge when seasoned with salt and pepper. For a gentle taste, use kosher salt or sea salt and for sharpness, apply freshly ground pepper. But experiment with other seasonings too. Zucchini is brightened by lemon and carrots can be deepened with thyme. Dried herbs are fine—in fact, I find them preferable.

Pre-Made Salad Mixes–Ready-to-eat salad mixes make eating healthy incredibly easy. If you're in a hurry on a weeknight and need a healthy side to go with dinner it's always nice to have bagged salad mix in the fridge at your disposal. They will keep for about a week.

Cooked Veggies–Around our house we always prep vegetables at the beginning of the week so that way they are easy to add to dishes when we need them. Our go to mix include bell peppers, mushrooms and onions. But really, the options are limitless and based on what you use the most of.

Mexican Quinoa

Ingredients:

- 2 garlic cloves, minced
- 1 C quinoa, rinse and drain
- 3 jalapeños, seeds and ribs removed, finely chopped
- 14.5 Oz can of diced tomatoes, with juices
- 15 Oz can black beans, drained and rinsed
- 1 1/4 C chicken broth
- 1/2 t salt
- 1 C frozen corn
- 1/3 C fresh parsley
- 2 t olive oil
- 2-3 t fresh lime juice

Preparation:

1. Add olive oil to saucepan and heat it medium flame.
2. When the oil shimmers, add the garlic and jalapenos. Cook for about 1 minute.
3. Stir in the quinoa, chicken broth, black beans, corn, tomatoes and salt. Cook mixture until boiling, cover, and cook until the liquid has been absorbed.
4. Take the pan off the heat and stir in the parsley and lime juice (begin with 2 tsp, then taste to decide if you want more).
5. Season with additional salt or pepper if needed.

To freeze: Freeze in an airtight container.

To use: When you're ready to serve, pop in the oven until the dish is heated through. Serve with cheese, sour cream and salsa.

Baked Ziti With Roasted Veggies

Ingredients:

- 1lb ziti
- 3 C roasted vegetables
- 1 T fresh parsley, finely chopped
- 3 C Pasta sauce
- 2 C mozzarella cheese

Preparation:

1. Place the pasta in boiling water. Cook until done, about 10 minutes. Take care not to overcook the pasta.
2. Drain the ziti right away.
3. Add vegetables of your choice (cauliflower, broccoli, zucchini, carrots, squash, beans, peas, etc.). Cover mixture completely with sauce.
4. Place foil or plastic wrap over the bowl and leave for 5 minutes or more.
5. Keep the cheese and parsley for garnishing when eating it.

To freeze: Cool it completely before packing it for freezing.

To use: Transfer it to a baking dish, cover with cheese and parley. Put in fridge or freeze it until you are ready to serve it.

Vegetable Soup

Ingredients:

- 1 C orzo pasta
- 1 onion, diced
- 1 C diced carrots
- 1/3 C balsamic vinegar
- 1 t olive oil
- 1 yellow squash, chopped
- 4 C chicken stock
- 1/4 C minced fresh parsley
- 2 garlic cloves, minced
- 1 C cooked navy beans
- 1 T honey
- 1/3 C grated Parmesan cheese
- 1/2 t black pepper
- 1/8 t salt

Preparation:

1. In a baking dish with a lid, combine the carrots, onions, squash, corn, oil and vinegar. Stir over medium heat for about 5 minutes till the onions become soft.
2. Add stock, beans, pasta and garlic and boil.
3. Cook mixture 15 minutes on medium heat, or till the pasta is soft enough.

4. Add the honey, parsley, salt, and pepper. Stir mixture vigorously and garnish the servings with some parmesan cheese on top.

To freeze: cool and pack the soup in freezable container.

To use: Place in fridge overnight to thaw. Pour contents in saucepan. Stir often on low heat for 13-17 minutes, or till hot.

Cheese Stuffed Peppers

Ingredients:

- 4 red peppers, large
- 1/2 C chopped onions
- 1 C shredded cheddar cheese
- 1 C bread crumbs
- 1/4 C low-fat ricotta cheese
- 2 T chicken stock
- 1/2 C frozen peas
- 1/2 C shredded mozzarella cheese
- 4 garlic cloves, minced
- 2 T grated Parmesan cheese
- 1 T minced fresh basil

Preparation:

1. Preheat oven to 350°F. Prepare peppers by slicing off tops and set aside. De-seed and place peppers in a baking dish with cut side up.
2. In a bowl, mix together the cheddar, bread crumbs, peas, onions, ricotta, mozzarella, stock, basil, and garlic. Mix well and fill the peppers with this mixture. Top with Parmesan.
3. Cover with pepper tops & bake 20 minutes until the peppers are somewhat soft. Take out of oven and remove tops off of the peppers and discard.

4. Bake for another 10 minutes until tops are golden brown.

To freeze: Put cooked cooled peppers in one layer in freezable container.

To use: Put in fridge to thaw and microwave for about 8 minutes, until hot.

Basil and Vegetable Soup

Ingredients:

- 1/4 C grated Parmesan cheese
- 1 medium sized tomato, diced
- 1/3 C green beans, diced
- 1 C chopped onions
- 1 small yellow squash, chopped
- 4 C chicken stock
- 1/4 C parsley, chopped
- 1/4 C diced celery
- 1/4 C breadcrumbs
- 1/4 C spaghetti
- 1/2 C chopped fresh basil
- 1 T tomato paste
- 1 t oil
- 3 garlic cloves, minced

Preparation:

1. Fry the onions till until they become golden brown or around 10 minutes.
2. Add the squash, tomatoes, celery, beans and a cup of stock. Stir until the veggies become soft, about 10 minutes.

3. Add the spaghetti, parsley, tomato paste, and the rest of the chicken stock and boil. Stir often and cook for about 15 minutes—until the spaghetti is soft enough.
4. In a food processor, add the Parmesan, bread crumbs, basil, and garlic. Make a paste and add to the liquid mixture. Stir well.

To freeze: cool the soup and pack in a freezable container.

To use: Place in fridge overnight to thaw. Move to a saucepan when ready to eat and cover it and stir frequently until hot.

Vegetables and Chili

Ingredients:

- 1 garlic clove, minced
- 1 T chili powder
- 2 t oregano
- 2 t ground cumin
- 1/8 t cayenne pepper
- 1 small zucchini, chopped
- 1 small red pepper, chopped
- 1 small yellow squash, chopped
- 2, 10 Oz cans dice tomatoes with green Chile peppers
- 1 C corn
- 2 T tomato paste
- 1 can rinsed cooked kidney beans
- 1 can rinsed cooked black beans
- 2 T olive oil
- Salt and pepper to taste

Preparation:

1. Add oil to Dutch oven and cook over medium heat.
2. Next, put in the onion and cook until soft, about 5 minutes.
3. Add chilli powder, garlic, oregano, cayenne and cumin, cooking until it's fragrant.

4. Add in the yellow squash, zucchini and red pepper, cook until soft, about 10 minutes.
5. Add the tomato paste, tomatoes, corn, and the beans.
6. Bring it to boil and then turn down to low. Let mixture simmer for about 20 minutes.
7. Add salt and pepper.

Freeze in an airtight freezer compatible container bag.

To cook, thaw and reheat over medium heat.

Vegetable Jambalaya Casserole

Ingredients:

- 1 bell pepper, diced
- 1 onion, diced
- 1 C uncooked long grain rice
- 3 cloves garlic, minced
- 1/2 C chopped celery
- 8 Oz tomato sauce
- 14 Oz diced tomatoes, un-drained
- 2 C water
- 1/8 t fennel seeds, crushed
- 1/2 t dried Italian seasoning
- 1/4 t crushed red pepper flakes
- 15 Oz red beans, drain and rinse
- 15 Oz butter beans, drain and rinse
- 1 T cooking oil

Preparation:

1. Heat oil over medium heat in a large skillet.
2. Sauté the bell pepper, onion, garlic and celery until tender or about 5 minutes, stirring often.
3. Add water, tomato sauce, tomatoes, red pepper flakes, Italian seasoning and fennel.

4. Add rice and boil. Reduce heat and cover, simmering for roughly 20-25 minutes until rice is soft. Stir often.
5. Throw in the beans and put lid back on. Keep simmering for an additional 10 minutes, stirring frequently.

To freeze: Place in fridge and cool, then put in freezer safe containers.

To eat: Place the frozen casserole in a pan and heat on low, stirring often until hot.

Chili Rice Casseroles

Ingredients:

- 3 C undercooked white rice
- 2 eggs, beaten
- 1-1/2 C sour cream
- 1/2 C of milk
- 2 C shredded Monterey Jack cheese
- 4 Oz chopped green chilies or jalapenos
- Salt and pepper to taste

Preparation:

1. Preheat the oven to 350.
2. Undercook rice by 5 minutes.
3. Mix the sour cream, rice, eggs, milk, chilies, 1-1/2 cups cheese, and salt and pepper to taste in a big bowl. Place in a greased 2 quarts glass baking dish and cover with some cheese.
4. Bake for 40-45 minutes until done.

To freeze: Cool in fridge. Transfer to freezable containers.

To eat: Thaw in fridge overnight. Before baking stir well and bake for about an hour until brown.

Noodle Casserole with Sour Cream

Ingredients:

- 1 ¼ lb ground beef
- 15 Oz tomato sauce
- 8 Oz egg noodles
- 1/2 t salt
- 1 ¼ C cottage cheese
- ½ C sour cream
- 1 C shredded cheddar cheese
- 1/2 C diced green onions (to taste)
- Black pepper

Preparation:

1. Preheat the oven to 350.
2. Put beef in a big skillet.
3. Drain fat, add 1/2 teaspoon salt, tomato sauce, and some fresh black pepper (ground).
4. Stir and let simmer while you get other Ingredients: ready.
5. Cook noodles. Drain and then keep aside.
6. Combine the cottage cheese and sour cream in a medium bowl.
7. Add some black pepper to taste.
8. Add in the noodles and then stir.
9. Throw in the green onion and mix until well combined.

10. Add half of your noodles to a glass baking dish. Put half of meat mixture on top, then half the cheese. Repeat again with remaining Ingredients.

Follow the packing instructions properly in the first chapter and freeze.

Fish Recipes

Fish can be a very healthy part of a well-balanced diet. The omga-3 fatty acids found in a large selection of fish and seafood are vital to our health. We have to consume these fatty acids from our food, as our bodies don't produce these.

Fish such as salmon contain an abundant amount of Omega 3's. Fish are also one of the cleanest most bioavailable sources of protein. From a health standpoint, evidence suggests that fish is a much better option than other animal proteins.

Cod with Salsa Verde

A salsa of parsley, jalapeños capers and lemon keeps this baked cod moist and succulent in the freezer.

Ingredients:

- 4 cod filets
- ½ C green onions, diced
- 1/4 C minced onion
- 1/2 C fresh parsley, diced
- ¼ C lemon juice
- 1 T lemon juice
- 2 T zest of a lemon
- 2 t olive oil
- 4 garlic cloves, minced
- 2 t jalapenos, minced

Preparation:

1. Set oven on 400°F and put a 24" x 24" foil piece on a baking sheet.
2. Take a bowl and combine the parsley, scallions, lemon juice, onions, capers, oil, garlic and pepper and mix well.

3. Arrange all the cod on baking sheet in one layer. Add scallion mixture as a topping and fold the foil over cod to make a sealed pack.
4. Bake for about 10 minutes, until the fish's center is opaque. Insert a knife into a cutlet to check if it has been well cooked.

To freeze: Place in freezable containers.

To use: Put in fridge overnight and thaw. When ready to eat put in microwave for 5 minutes.

Sweet Sicilian Halibut

Ingredients:

- 4-6 Oz halibut steaks
- 3 C onions, chopped
- 3 T raisins
- 1 red bell pepper, diced
- 2 T white wine vinegar
- 2 t garlic, minced
- 1 drop hot sauce
- 2 T parsley, chopped
- 1 t olive oil
- 1 t dried oregano
- 1 t sugar
- 1/2 t salt

Preparation:

1. Spray a non-stick skillet with cooking spray and apply to medium heat until hot. Add onions, red peppers, and oil.
2. Cover and stir for 15 minutes, until the onions are golden brown.
3. Toss in the vinegar, garlic, sugar, hot sauce, oregano, and salt and stir well.

4. Put the halibut tight on the vegetables, cover then cook about 8 minutes, or till the center of the fish is opaque.

5. Sprinkle with parsley and serve.

To freeze: Place the cooked and cooled halibut in a freezer compatible container.

To use: Thaw in the fridge overnight and microwave for 3 to 5 minutes, or till hot.

Curry-spiced Seafood with Veggies and Rice

Ingredients:

- 1 C long grain white rice
- 1/2 C onions, minced
- 1/2 C red peppers, minced
- 1/2 C carrots, shredded
- 1/2 C celery, minced
- 2 scallions, chopped
- 8 Oz cod fillets, cut into 1" cubes
- 4 Oz medium shrimp, deveined and peeled
- 2 T apple juice or white wine
- 2 t soy sauce
- 1 t garlic, minced
- 1/4 t curry powder
- 1/8 t salt

Preparation:

1. Cook rice as described on the package.
2. Spray a non-stick skillet with cooking spray and keep on med/high heat until the skillets hot.
3. Add the peppers, onions, celery, carrots and scallions. Stir until the vegetables are bright, should take 2 minutes, and place into a bowl.

4. To the heated skillet, add all the other Ingredients:. Including the shrimp, cod, apple juice or wine, garlic, soy sauce, salt, and curry powder. Cover it and stir for 4 to 6 minutes until the center of the fish and shrimp are opaque.

5. Toss the vegetables into the skillet with the rest of the Ingredients:. Heat and serve with the rice.

To freeze: Place the cooled rice in a freezer compatible container, and place the seafood and veggies on top.

To use: Thaw in the fridge overnight. Heat a saucepan and stir for 10 minutes or until hot.

Snack Recipes

Shrimp Puffs

Ingredients:

- 1lb shrimp, shelled and deveined
- 6 slices firm white sandwich bread
- 1-1/2 C Gruyere or Havarti cheese, shredded
- 3/4 C mayonnaise
- 2 cloves garlic, minced
- 1 t lemon zest
- Dash pepper
- 1 t dried dill weed
- 1 T olive oil
- 1 T butter

Preparation:

1. Preheat the oven to 300 degrees.
2. Cut out 4 circles from every slice of bread with a cookie cutter. Put them on a cookie sheet and bake them in oven until bread is dry and crisp, turning over halfway through baking. Cool them.

3. Heat olive oil and butter in a skillet and cook the shrimp with garlic until the shrimp start to curl and turn pink. Set aside for 10-15 minutes letting them cool slightly.
4. In large bowl, combine lemon zest, cheese, mayonnaise, pepper and dill. Finely chop the shrimp and add to the mixture.
5. Top the bread rounds with the shrimp mixture.
6. Now freeze on the baking sheet in a single layer, and keep them in a freezer container in a single layer as well.
7. When ready to eat, simply bake for 10-14 minutes at 400 degrees, or until they are golden brown.

Filo Onion Rolls

Ingredients:

- 2 C Gruyere or Swiss cheese, grated
- 8 Oz cream cheese, softened
- 9 (9" x 14") sheets filo dough, thawed
- 3 cloves garlic, minced
- 2 onions, chopped
- 1/2 t dried thyme leaves
- 1/4 C butter
- 1/3 C melted butter
- 1/8 t pepper

Preparation:

1. In a large bowl, mix the gruyere and cream cheese. Set mixture aside.
2. Take a skillet, sauté the onions in 1/4 cup butter continue sautéing them until they are very soft and browning. That should take close to 10 minutes. Mix in the garlic and cook for another minute. Cool for 20 minutes. Combine the cheese mixture with the onion, and mix well. Put in the fridge for 30 minutes.
3. Place a sheet of the dough on the a hard surface, brush the dough with melted butter, put another sheet on it, brush with butter, and finally put one more sheet on top.

4. Take the mixture, and make 3 rolls with three layers of dough for each roll. Roll up carefully, brush with butter. I recommend cutting the rolls in half, and placing 3 half rolls on separate cookie sheets. Cover tightly with plastic wrap and freeze overnight.
5. When eating, preheat oven to 375 degrees F. Cut the rolls into 1 inch pieces. Bake for 10-15 minutes, the rolls should be brown and the cheese filling should be melted. Let the rolls cool for 5 minutes, and enjoy!

Calzones

Ingredients:

- 16 un-risen dinner rolls, frozen (or frozen bread loaves)
- 1lb Italian sausage
- 2 eggs
- 1 medium onion, diced
- 1/4 t red pepper flakes
- 15 Oz ricotta cheese
- 1/2 t Italian seasoning
- 1/2 C Parmesan cheese, grated
- 1-1/2 C mozzarella cheese, grated
- 2 T parsley, chopped
- 1/2 t salt
- Black pepper to taste
- Marinara sauce, for serving
- 1 T butter
- 1 egg, beaten

Preparation:

1. Thaw frozen rolls on a baking sheet. Cover with a towel and let rolls rise for 2 - 3 hours.
2. Melt butter in a heated skillet on medium heat.
3. Add onion and cook for a few minutes.

4. Add the sausage to the skillet and cook until brown. Crumble the sausage while stirring.
5. Add some Italian seasoning and flakes of red pepper. Remove the mixture and cool it.
6. In a bowl, mix Parmesan, ricotta, mozzarella, salt, 2 eggs, pepper, and parsley. Once the sausage is cooled, mix it in and set aside.
7. Once rolls have risen, roll them until thin as paper on a lightly floured hard surface.
8. Put 3-4 Tablespoons of the filling onto one half of the circle of dough and fold it over, sealing edges by pressing together.
9. Cover tightly with foil and freeze.
10. When ready to eat, thaw overnight in the refrigerator.
11. Preheat the oven to 400 degrees.
12. Brush the calzone with the beaten egg.
13. Bake for 10-14 minutes, until golden brown.
14. Serve with your favorite marinara sauce.

Jalapeno Poppers

Ingredients:

- 3 Oz Pepper jack cheese, softened
- 8 Oz cream cheese, softened
- 2 t chili powder
- 1 t oregano leaves, dried
- 25 jalapeno peppers, cut in half, de-seeded
- 2 C Pepper Jack cheese, shredded
- 1 C flour
- 3/4 C milk
- 1 egg, beaten
- 1/2 t salt
- 1-1/2 C dried breadcrumbs
- Oil for frying

Preparation:

1. Combine chilli powder, oregano, pepper jack cheese, and cream cheese in a bowl and mix well.
2. Take the pepper halves, and blanch them in water for a couple of minutes, then drain and finally dry completely with towels.
3. Fill the halves of jalapeno pepper with the cheese mixture.
4. Combine milk and egg in a bowl and mix flour and salt in another. Dip the jalapenos into the bowl with milk first and then the one with the flour. Make sure to coat completely. Now

put the jalapenos on racks and dry them for roughly 10 minutes.
5. Next submerge the jalapenos in the milk mixture again and toss them in the breadcrumbs.
6. Dry them for 30-40 minutes, and if desired dip them in the milk mixture and breadcrumbs again if you want a thicker coating.
7. If freezing don't fry the peppers. Place them on a cookie sheet then put them in the freezer until hard. At that point place them in single layers in freezer containers.
8. When ready to eat simply place them on a cookie sheet and bake for 20-30 minutes at 350 degrees. They are ready when golden and crispy.
9. You can also choose to fry them. Heat oil in a large skillet to 365 degrees. Deep fry them for 3-5 minutes. They will be golden and delicious. Drain the excess oil on paper towels.

Red and White Tortellini

Ingredients:

- 2 (18 Oz) pkgs. Uncooked refrigerated/frozen cheese tortellini or ravioli
- 1 C shredded Parmesan or mozzarella cheese
- 12 Oz jar four cheese Alfredo sauce
- 28 Oz packed spaghetti sauce
- Some meatballs
- 3 T milk
- 1/2 C water

Preparation:

1. Preheat your oven to 350 degrees
2. In a glass 3 quart baking dish, layer the spaghetti sauce and the tortellini. Add water to the emptied sauce jar, shake and pour on the tortellini.
3. Empty the alfredo sauce on the dish. Place milk in the empty Alfredo sauce jar, and pour the mixture all over the dish. You can now top the dish with frozen meatballs if you want. Sprinkle it with some cheese.
4. Cover with aluminium foil then bake for 50-60 minutes in the preheated oven. Remove the foil and bake another 10 minutes.
5. Freeze in an appropriate container, heat for 20-30 minutes in a 350 degree oven to eat.

Dessert Recipes

Tips for freezing and thawing desserts

Always completely cool any dessert before wrapping it and freezing it. Wrapping or covering a warm cake or tart will encourage condensation and makes for a soggy texture and freezer burn.

Always double-wrap your frozen desserts. First wrap the dessert in multiple layers of plastic wrap—at least two and then put in a Ziploc bag or freezable container. Gently push out as much air as possible.

Depending on how much time you have, you may thaw your dessert in the fridge or even on the counter. As long as I have the time, I prefer to un-wrap the tart or cake, put it on a serving plate, loosely cover it with plastic wrap, and then thaw it in the fridge.

Mud Pie - Mocha edition

Ingredients:

- 9 inch premade chocolate pie crust
- 1 pint of your favorite brand of chocolate ice cream, softened
- 1 pint coffee ice cream, softened
- 2 T chopped almonds
- 1 Oz jar hot fudge sauce

Preparation:

1. Spread the ice cream onto the crust. Spread over it about 1 C of warmed up fudge sauce, cover dessert and then freeze until firm.
2. Next, put coffee ice cream over the frozen dessert, then warm remaining hot fudge sauce and gently top the pie with it, drizzling as you go.
3. Sprinkle pie with the almonds and then cover it tightly and freeze for 2 hours (at least and more if possible) before serving.
4. Remove dessert from the freezer about 5 minutes before you intend to serve it.

Pumpkin Pie

Ingredients:

- 1 prepared piecrust
- 3/4 C honey
- 2 C 100% pumpkin puree
- 1/2 t salt
- 1 t cinnamon
- 1/4 t ground cloves
- 1/2 t ground ginger
- 1 t ground nutmeg
- 2 eggs, beaten
- 1 ½ C milk

Preparation:

1. Put all Ingredients: into a large bowl and mix together well.
2. Next, pour all the mixture into your pie crust.
3. Put pie in oven and bake the pie at 425 degrees F for about 15 minutes. After that, reduce oven temperature to 350 and continue baking for an additional 30-40 minutes, until pie is done in middle.

To freeze: Completely cool the pie before you wrap and freeze it. If you're freezing it whole it's best to use a pie pan made of glass. Sometimes, I find it is easier to cut into slices before you freeze.

For eating: Thaw it and then bake at 350 F for 50-60 minutes until warmed.

The pie filling and crust can be frozen separately and thawed before you pour in the filling and bake it as usual.

Strawberry Lemon Mousse Tartlets

Ingredients:

- 9 tartlet shells, graham cracker crust
- 8 Oz package of cream cheese, softened
- 1 ½ C strawberry sherbet
- 7 T freshly squeezed lemon juice
- 1, 14 Oz can condensed milk, sweetened

Preparation:

1. First, soften sherbet at room temperature for about 15 minutes. After it is soft, stir to make it workable and easy to use.
2. Place tartlet shells on your work table.
3. Fill the shells with gelato. Be careful because you can damage the crusts quite easily. Freeze them for about 40 minutes.
4. Beat the cream cheese with mixer until smooth and creamy. Gradually add in condensed milk and make a smooth mix. Slowly mix in lemon juice. The mixture will now thicken.
5. Fill the tartlet shells with the mixture. Freeze for at least 3 hours.

To freeze: Store in the freezer as directed at the beginning of this section.

To eat: Remove from fridge 20-30 minutes before you serve.

Coffee Almond Tart

Ingredients:

- 1 10 inch pie crust
- 1/3 C melted butter
- 18 Oreos, crushed
- 2 C chocolate ice cream, softened
- 1 quart coffee flavored ice cream, softened
- 1 C hot fudge sauce
- 1/3 C toasted almonds, sliced

Preparation:

1. Mix the crushed up Oreos and butter (melted) and spread over both sides of 10" pie crust. Freeze for 15 minutes.
2. Spread both kinds of ice cream into the pie crust and then sprinkle with the almonds.

To freeze: Store in the freezer for 3 hours or more.

To eat: Remove from freezer at least 15 minutes before you serve. Serve with warmed fudge sauce.

Breakfast Recipes

Stuffed Italian Burgers

Ingredients:

- 2 cloves garlic, minced
- 1/2 pkg. frozen spinach, thawed
- ½ t salt
- ½ t pepper
- 1 T fresh parsley, chopped
- ¼ C Italian bread crumbs
- ¼ C Parmesan, grated
- 2 slices ham
- 1lblean ground beef, or veal
- 1 egg
- 2 slices of cheese, provolone is best

Preparation:

1. Combine the de-thawed spinach and half half the garlic, pepper and salt and set them aside.
2. In another bowl, beat the egg, stir in the Italian bread crumbs, parsley Parmesan cheese and the remaining pepper, salt and garlic. Add the meat and mix until combined.

3. Place the ham on the cutting board, top each slice with a cheese slice, and half the spinach mixture. Roll it up and cut into half.
4. Shape the meat mixture into four equal sized patties around the ham.

To freeze: Layer the patties between sheets of waxed paper and store in an airtight container in freezer for up to one month.

To use: Thaw patties in fridge. Grill on medium heat. Turn only once.

Apricot and Raisin Oatmeal

Ingredients:

- ¼ C milk
- 1 C old-fashioned rolled oats
- 2 T dried apricots, chopped
- 2 T raisins
- 1/8 t ground nutmeg
- 2 T roasted almonds, chopped

Preparation:

1. Prepare your oats as indicated on packaging and divide into two individual sized bowls.
2. Cover with raisins, milk, almonds, apricots and nutmeg.

For directions in freezing and eating, please follow the instructions at the beginning of the desserts section.

Hearty & Healthy Blueberry Muffins

Ingredients:

- 1 ¼ C flour, whole wheat
- 1 Cold-fashioned oats
- 2 C blueberries, fresh work best
- ¼ C pecans
- ¼ C ground flaxseed
- 1 t baking soda
- 1 t baking powder
- 1/2 t salt
- ½ C light brown sugar
- 1 C plain Greek yogurt
- 3 T butter, melted
- 1 T orange zest
- ¼ C fresh squeezed orange juice
- 1 egg
- 1 t vanilla

Preparation:

1. Set oven temperature to 375° F. Line a standard sized muffin tin with paper liners. In your food processor, combine the oats, flour, pecans, flaxseed meal, baking powder, salt and baking soda until powdery.

2. In mixing bowl, mix together the sugar, yogurt, butter, orange zest, egg, juice, and vanilla extract. Stir in flour mixture and combine well. Fold in the blueberries.
3. Empty batter into the muffin cups and spread evenly. Muffins are done once a toothpick can be inserted and come out clean, around 20-25 minutes.

For directions in freezing and eating, please follow the instructions at the beginning of the desserts section.

Conclusion

As I'm sure you've noticed, with freezer meals your cooking methods don't really change. What changes are the steps you take after the initial cooking process. There is one aspect of make ahead freezer meals that needs to be quickly discussed. I am talking about keeping an inventory, expiration date, and instructions to thaw and heat. These three things are important to getting the most out of your make ahead meals.

Since most cooked meals expire between a few days and 3 months from the date of cooking, it is important to write down the date of expiration.

When I cook more than 25 dishes, I always keep a list of dates for when they are put in the freezer. When I take out any food, I mark it off on the list. For example, if there are 5 chicken casseroles and I take out one, I always mark on the list that there are 4 left. How does this help? It lets me know when I need to cook again. Using this system my family never goes hungry—especially on those nights when we don't have anything planned.

By utilizing the steps and tips in this book, you will be much more prepared for anything unexpected that life has to throw your way. Your family will always have options if you're working late, or you can even portion things according to single servings so that if you're home alone you can quickly have a healthy and nutritious dinner prepared with little effort on your part.

Thanks for reading. If you're interested in learning more about prepping and storing food be sure to check out my book 'Canning and Preserving: Your Quick and Easy Guide to Fresh Food All Year Long.'

Printed in Great Britain
by Amazon